This edition is published by special arrangement with
HarperCollins*Children'sBooks*, a division of HarperCollins Publishers, Inc.

Grateful acknowledgment is made to HarperCollins*Children'sBooks*,
a division of HarperCollins Publishers, Inc. for permission to reprint *Sid and Sam*
by Nola Buck, illustrated by G. Brian Karas. Text copyright © 1996
by Nola Buck; illustrations copyright © 1996 by G. Brian Karas.

Printed in the United States of America

ISBN 0-15-314264-2

3 4 5 6 7 8 9 10   060   02 01 00

Sid and Sam

by Nola Buck
pictures by G. Brian Karas

Harcourt

Orlando   Boston   Dallas   Chicago   San Diego

Visit *The Learning Site!*
www.harcourtschool.com

Sid saw Sam.

Sam saw Sid.

"Please sing," said Sid.

"Sing a song, Sam."

"Sure thing," said Sam.

"I will sing."

Sam sang.

Sam sang a long song.

Sid sang along with Sam.

"Sing slower, Sid," Sam said.

Sid sang slower.

"Sing softer, Sid," Sam said.

Sid sang softer.

"Sing lower, Sid," Sam said.

Sid sang lower.

Sid sang low.

Sid sang so low.

"Stop, Sid.

Please stop," Sam said.

"Sure, Sam," said Sid.
"I will stop."

"Soon, Sid?" Sam said.

"Soon?"

"Soon, Sam," Sid said.
"Soon."

Sid sang a new song.

Sid sang, and sang,
and sang.

"Sid," Sam said.

"That song is so long "

"So long?" said Sid.

"So long," Sam said.

"So long, Sid!"

"See you soon!"